THE SHORT, QUICK, BEGINNER'S PREPPER MANUAL
GETTING YOURSELF PREPPED IN 30 DAYS OR LESS

BY
KARL A.D. BROWN

This book is dedicated to my son Hugo.

Foreword

Welcome and congratulations on your decision to be become more self-reliant in an emergency. This beginner emergency guide was created out of alarm and concern for what has now become the new normal. We can't switch on the television anymore without seeing a report of a terrorist attack, mass casualty shooting, or weather-related calamity going on somewhere in the world. This short manual is a very quick guide for any individual who wants to be prepared to react and bunker in for at least 30 days. This booklet is not just written for "preppers" or those in the survival community. It was written to give a solid starting point for anyone who is new to the topic of emergency preparedness and has some concerns about the personal safety of themselves and their families. Maybe you or someone you know has been sitting on the fence, and you would like to give them a little motivation to get themselves prepping. This short pamphlet is perfect because it is quick and to the point. It provides clear, easy, instructions on how to get started.

For many reading this pamphlet, this will be the beginning of an important life conversation. This short manual is a guide to navigate that conversation and the decision to have an emergency preparedness plan in place. Maybe there are people you know who are wavering on whether to begin preparing. Maybe it all seems overwhelming, or they are afraid to ask questions out of fear. Maybe they do believe that in an emergency, the government and their fellow man will see them and their family through, but you can possibly convince them that their chance for survival goes up if they are also prepared. Have them download a copy of this manual. I encourage all readers of this manual to leave their own thoughts, hints, and advice, either in their reviews or in discussion forums on this booklet. You will sound the alarm and provide great advice for those who are just beginning their prepping journey.

This booklet is not a know-all and do-all about prepping; there are other, more detailed books available for that. Instead it is a reasoned, short and pointed, beginning guide for the person who is new to the preparedness lifestyle. This booklet was created so it could be easily downloaded to your reading device and read quickly, so that you can get yourself going in a few hours after browsing through some, if not all, of the chapters. If after reading this manual and you determine that you need more in depth information for longer term planning some great books are: *The Prepper's Blueprint: The Step-By-Step Guide To Help You Through Any Disaster* by Tess Pennington, and *When The Grid Goes Down, Disaster Preparations and Survival Gear For Making Your Home Self-Reliant* by Tony Nester.

There are a lot of know-it-alls in the preparedness community, and I am not one of them. I am not going to tell you that I know everything about prepping. On the contrary, I am here to say I am like the average person who will probably be reading this manual. I am an ordinary person, not particularly political or religious. I am just a concerned father who has watched as the situation in our country and around the world has gotten alarmingly worse over the course of the last few years, and, because I have a family, I have had to think about the unthinkable. I have realized that I need an emergency plan in place, just in case something occurs that would require me to figure out where my family members are, make sure that we all make it home safe and then stay home, and hopefully out of the way, until the situation has passed. I figure a lot of concerned Americans are now thinking the same thing.

The preparations discussed in this manual should be able to get you through the initial stages of an emergency, regardless of whether it happens to be weather-related or a social disruption. Let's look at weather emergencies. You should always prepare for the usual natural emergencies where you reside. Depending on where you live it might be hurricanes, tornadoes, earthquakes, flooding, forest fires, or snow storms. Social disruptions include a terrorist attack, riot, shelter in place, or martial law. If you have been like me, watching all the scary reports on the news, seeing people run for their lives, then you know that the world is a dangerous place, and that bad things do happen to good people. The question is, if an emergency occurred where you live or work, would you be ready to act?

One way to look at it is if you have been preparing yourself, then you will find that when an emergency occurs, you will be able to respond in a positive way. It's like muscle memory. Because you have been turning over emergency scenarios in your head routinely, when the day comes and you have to act, you will be able to respond. If you have an emergency plan in place, you will be able to follow through and get yourself and your family to safety.

Chapter One: Getting Started on Your Own Personal Emergency Preparedness Journey

So how do I begin? If you are reading this and prepping for the first time, then this is where millions of preppers have been in the past. The question is, what are you really prepping for? That is the question you must ask yourself. Get yourself a composition book, or open up Microsoft Word, and write it down. Next you have to ask yourself what type of prep it will be, either "bugging in" which is prepper jargon for staying in your home, or "bugging out," which means going to a safety location that is not your primary residence.

Most plans will have a combination of both of these two scenarios. Since most emergencies occur during work hours, and school hours for those with children, the most likely scenario will be that your family is dispersed when the emergency occurs. The other scenario could be that you are home when the crisis happens and you will have to put your emergency plans into play.

Let's look at scenario (1) Bugging In: You are at work and the emergency erupts. Do all your family members know the plan for such an emergency? How do you get the children home safely? How do you get home safely? Do you know all possible routes to your home from where you work? What if you cannot drive your car and have to walk home? Do you know the safest, quietest route home? (The one where you will run into the least amount of people). So the emergency plays out something like this: The emergency takes place, family plan kicks in, kids dropped off at home, perhaps by you or your spouse, and you or your spouse find your way home. If you are single, then for you it might be just getting to your safety location and bugging in.

Here's a look at scenario (2) Bugging Out: You are at work and the emergency erupts. Do all your family members know the plan for such an emergency? Who picks up the kids, and do you meet at home or at a preplanned location? Where is your bug out gear located? Is it at home or in your car? The same questions that were asked above apply here as well. Do you know the safest and quietest way both to your home and your safety location? What if you cannot drive your car and you have to walk? You should have a plan in place so that you can make it to your bug out location as quickly and expeditiously as possible.

The safety location should have all you need to survive for at least 30 days or more. It should minimize your exposure to any threats that might be present. So, that's the first thing you should be thinking about. What am I preparing for? This is an important question that can orient you on your way to being prepared. This question will have you prepare according to the perceived emergency, and some things will naturally get prioritized over others.

Once you have established what it is you are prepping for, you have to take stock of your safety location. Do you live in a detached house, apartment, RV, condominium, or boat? For anyone who is planning to go seriously off the grid, your safety location could be a cave, camouflaged tent, or boat. How much space do you have to store food, fuel, medical supplies, and anything else you might need to see you through the emergency? The first thing you should do is give your safety location a thorough cleaning. If you live in an apartment or a detached house, you should go through all your stuff, get rid of anything you do not need, keeping in mind that you are now creating storage space for the necessities for your family and yourself. Clean out your cabinets, and if you find any old or expired food or medicine, get rid of it. Clean your car as well, going through your trunk and any storage spaces.

On the planning timeline, you have (1) identified the situation you are prepping for, and (2) taken stock of your safety location and given it a thorough cleaning from top to bottom.

Here are some possible emergencies, and maybe there is one or more on the list that you have decided to prepare for: (1) Terrorist Attack, (2) Economic Collapse, (3) Pandemic or, (4) Natural Disaster. It is important to note that each of the general emergencies above can be further broken down. For example, a terrorist attack could come in the form of a mass shooting, bombing, or some other type of radioactive, biological, or chemical attack. A terrorist could also take down the electrical grid. If a foreign government wanted to cause mischief, they could detonate a small nuclear bomb in the atmosphere and cause an EMP (Electromagnetic Pulse), which would take out the grid and most of our electronics. A natural disaster could be a wildfire, flood, winter storm, hurricane, drought, earthquake, or tornado. What you prep for is also a matter of common sense and shrewd judgment. If you live in a rural area, then you might not rank a terror threat as high as, say, a weather-related emergency. **In these times, a person living in a high-density area, a major city or large town, is likely to rank a terror attack higher up on their list of possible threats**. Keep in mind that if there is an attack in and around your neighborhood or close to where you work, the authorities will most likely issue a shelter in place advisory and seal off the area.

This leads us to your safety location. Where is it situated? If you are the average person who is just trying to make ends meet, then most likely the only place you have available to you is your home. Where do you live? Is it rural or urban? What's your neighborhood like? Is it generally a safe or high crime area? Do you know your neighbors, and do they know you? What are your neighbors like? Are they good people, or can you not trust them? How much privacy do you have in your safety location? Do you have roommates, or do you live alone? Are you sharing your apartment, but you have your own room? Do you have your own home and complete privacy, or do you have a bug out location on another property that is not your primary residence? Your safety location is important because that is where you and your family will have to bunker in until the threat passes or subsides.

Although this book's main focus is bunkering in at your safety location, a few words must be said about the possibility of the emergency occurring in your immediate vicinity, and you become caught up in it. In this new world of deadly rampages and terrorism, preppers have to develop a keen sense of situational awareness. When you enter any gun free zone where there are a lot of people, you should make sure you know where all the exits are located. You should also make sure you are constantly on the lookout for a good place to take cover and stay concealed if the unthinkable was to happen. When you go to a concert or the cinema, think of what might be the best seat or area to be in if some maniac started shooting. It is up to you to be constantly vigilant, and you should make it a habit to run those scenarios through your head. It might just save the lives of your loved ones and yourself. Some great books to read on how to survive an active shooter situation are the following: *Staying Alive: How to Act Fast and Survive Deadly Encounters* by Michael Dorn, *100 Deadly Skills: The SEAL Operative's Guide to Eluding Pursuers, Evading Capture, and Surviving Any Dangerous Situation* by Clint Emerson, and the *SAS Survival Handbook, Third Edition: The Ultimate Guide to Surviving Anywhere* by John Wiseman.

People will say that this kind of thinking is all doom and gloom. They will also say you should not live in fear, that you should hold your head high and go about your life and not let the bad people control you, because then they have won. There is some truth to that, but we can't stick our heads in the sand and deny reality. It is good to be brave, but it's better to be brave with supplies, skills, and grit. Recognizing the harsh realities of the world is common sense, pragmatic, and ultimately optimistic, because what you are trying to do is to keep your loved ones and yourself safe until the threat is gone. Do not let anyone make you feel bad because you are looking out for you and your family's wellbeing. This is not about political or peer pressure. This is about survival. Every person has the right to ensure to the best of their ability that they are prepared to help themselves in an emergency, and not be a burden on the emergency services personnel who will be overwhelmed by the grasshoppers who did not prepare. Let them take their chances with survival; you should not.

So at this point in your planning, you have a clear idea of what you are prepping for, and you have also checked out and evaluated your safety location. You have also begun to do something you may not have been doing before; you shifted gears mentally and have begun to think like a prepper. You have started to look at your environment and the people around you in a new way. Thinking like this in this new world, where so many people are devising ways to hurt others, is now a necessity. Gone are the days when we could pretty much abdicate the responsibility of our personal safety to the police and the government. For some of you reading this manual, this will be the first time you have decided to shoulder that responsibility, and you will find that it is very empowering.

Chapter Two: Developing a Quick Emergency Plan

Now that you have established the threat that you would like to prepare for, and you have proven the viability of your safety location, you need to get a cohesive plan together. If you have a family, whether you are the mom or dad, you have to get everyone on board. There will be people who will be uncomfortable with prepping because it has gotten such a bad rap in the media. Preppers are usually portrayed as crazy people who hate the government. Nothing could be more misleading. Most preppers, you will find out, are normal, ordinary people. You will find that preppers are a diverse bunch. The lifestyle demographics will cover all political leanings, sexual orientation, religions, and racial lines. Old and young, married and single, people are waking up and realizing that they have to put something aside and be prepared for that Black Swan event that might be just over the horizon. If you are new to prepping, you will find in this manual a few terms and resources that are well known in prepper circles. Highlight and do a web search on them.

Now you need to get your to-do list in order. You have cleaned out and arranged your safety location, and now you will have to stock it and get you and your family thinking clearly.

Here is an example of what your initial list might look like: (1) Talk with family about having a safety plan. (2) Draw up the safety plan with spouse. (3) Clean and organize safety location. (4) Stock safety location with supplies. (5) Prep vehicles. (6) Have a list of emergency phone numbers and radio channels. (7) Scout out immediate neighbors. (8) Have copies of all important papers in a hidden location. (9) Make sure all home and car insurances are up to date. (10) Have extra cash on hand in home. (11) Harden safety location. (12) Understand and learn basic self-defense. (13) Make family decision on firearms. (14) Run a few drills to ensure everyone has an idea of what to do if an emergency occurs.

A list like this is important. Have it before you chat with your other family members, because when they see how organized you are, it makes it easier for them to see that you have a coherent safety plan. Talk with them about the emergency you are prepping for, and you will find that preparing in this way will overlap with other possible emergencies. Something else could occur, not necessarily what you had prepared for, but because you had a plan in place and you were thinking like a prepper, your ability to safely survive the emergency will be greater. You have to make sure you know your family and yourself well. Understand everyone's strengths and weaknesses, mental and physical limitations. Show your list to your spouse. What, if anything, would they have an issue with? Find out and discuss, get everything out into the open before you begin. If your spouse believes that you are overreacting, even after presenting a well thought-out safety plan, ask them if you can go ahead anyway, just in case, and keep them apprised of all your accomplishments and important developments.

One significant part of prepping is understanding that successful preppers are very careful with their money. If you are in debt, figure out the quickest way to get out of it and begin immediately. Try not to acquire any new debt. Preppers do not live beyond their means. Start putting your money aside, and save, save, save. Decide what's really necessary in your life, and do more with less. Even if you are struggling to make ends meet, you will find that there are many preppers out there who are poor but still manage to put an extra can of hash away in their pantry. Remember the golden rule of prepping: Blend in and do not draw attention to yourself. You now need to become a chameleon. Remember that just because you have become aware of possible threats and your need to prepare for them, this does not mean you need to start behaving in any way that makes you stand out in your community. That is also a conversation that you will have to have with your family.

At the beginning, you will have an important question to ask yourself. Are you going to keep your preps secret, or will you get others involved? This is a fundamental decision that you will have to make, and it will be contingent on the relationships you have with others in your community. What would be safer and more advantageous to you? It could go either way, deciding to prep alone or with others. If you decide to keep your preps secret, then you need to stick with that decision, and your family members should understand that they should not discuss what they are doing with anyone else.

Who is in your group? You should have a clear idea of who will be involved in your safety plan. Remember, depending on the amount of people in the group, you will have to plan to feed and take care of those individuals during the emergency, and you need to have adequate supplies to do that. Make clear rules, write them down somewhere, and stick to them. Sit down with your family and discuss all the important decisions that you will need to make. Make it a family discussion; everyone gets a say. When a rule is made, write it down. This is the time to start keeping your **emergency binder**. You also need to have a clear and deep discussion about how you will respond if someone shows up on your doorstep during the emergency. Do you let them in, or do you tell them to go? There will be a lot of difficult decisions that will have to be made.

Make sure you have copies of all your important papers, wills, insurance, bank statements, marriage certificates, military discharge papers, firearms permits, deeds, and birth certificates buried or stored in a safe place that is accessible to only you or your spouse.

Now that you have made your plan and discussed it with your family, it's time to start stocking your pantry.

Chapter Three: Stocking Your Pantry

If you have cash on hand, one of the first things you have to do is begin to stock your pantry. Or just plain stock up on food stores. There are a few things you will need to think about first. A lot of people like to stock up on things they know they like to eat. This is a good idea, because when you are under stress, having something nice to eat can help to lift your spirits. Know your family's eating habits as well as your own. Stock up on those items, within reason. Remember you need to stock things that have a long shelf life. If you just want to follow the initial limits of this manual, which is to be completely self-sufficient for 30 days, then you need to understand how much food your family would need if they have three meals a day for 30 days. For a family of four, that's 12 meals in a day. These meals could be individually made, or you can make one big batch of food a day, with all meals coming from one pot.

Under stress and in some type of lockdown circumstances, one large pot of food that can keep for the day may be preferred. If there is no electricity to keep food cool, you may have to rethink the meal plan.

Let's begin thinking about what types of food should be stored. You need most of your survival food to be items with a long shelf life. A lot of canned food will have shelf lives of two to four years. When you shop, check the "use by" date. If the date is under a year, select other cans that are over a year. Here is a quick list of some supplies that might be a good starting foundation: Flour, sugar, rice, powdered potatoes, powdered milk, boxed UHT (ultra-high temperature) milk that can be stored without refrigeration, canned corned beef, soups, tuna, salmon, hash, canned vegetables—corn, tomatoes, spinach— coffee, tea, oatmeal, cornmeal, every spice you like, including, salt, pepper, garlic, and onion, also ketchup, honey, packaged meals like macaroni and cheese, soups, Raman noodles, olive oil, baking soda, baking powder, raisins, nuts, peanut butter, chocolate, cocoa powder, energy bars, bottled water, canned soda, powdered drink mixes. Most importantly and immediately, you will need water—**one gallon per person per day**. Water sometimes presents a problem for preppers. Absent a ready, fresh source, bottled water is something you may want to consider. Some preppers dig ponds, get an old fashioned pitcher hand pump installed, or they buy rain barrels to catch water. I left meat and perishable items for last, because if there is a loss of power and you do not have a way to keep your food refrigerated, then you face the dilemma of losing what's in your refrigerator. Always have a few bags of ice in your freezer. If you have a cooler, you might be able to keep your perishables cool for a few hours. Maybe these items would be the first for you to consume, so they do not go to waste. If you have the money, then you can get a generator powerful enough to run your refrigerator and your well pump, if you have a well. During an emergency, you don't need to light every room in your house or have every appliance running. You just need power to keep your food cool and your water on. Most people will lose water when the power goes out.

Remember to always rotate your stock. Put the items that expire first in front. You can use these items in your daily life, replacing as needed. You should look at your pantry as a place to store extra food that you actually use, and replenish. That way you have a working excess food supply. You get into the habit of rotating and adding to your excess stock. You also get a sense of what you and your family really need and like to eat. It's amazing the peace of mind a stocked pantry brings. You will never run out of the items you eat and use regularly.

Other things you can stock in your pantry, in addition to food supplies, are the following: tubes of toothpaste, duct tape, a good flashlight, water purification tablets, can opener, garbage bags, toilet paper, unscented soap, shampoo, deodorant, cough and flu medicine, feminine hygiene products, toilet paper, paper towels, hand sanitizer, extra batteries, and candles. If you have a baby, be sure to stock extra diapers, infant formula, and baby food. If you have pets, you should also stock some extra foods for them as well.

You can supplement your store-bought food with dehydrated long-term emergency food supplies. I have included the web addresses of a few companies from which you can purchase kits ranging from 1-week to 12-month food supplies:

www.wisefoodstorage.com/long-term-food-supply.html

www.myfoodstorage.com/long-term-food-storage.html

https://valleyfoodstorage.com/

Chapter Four: Medical Supplies

Make sure that you have on hand the necessary medical supplies you need for an extended period of time. In this manual we are planning for the initial 30 days. If you or a family member has a chronic condition, like asthma or diabetes, that requires prescription drugs, you need to have an emergency stash put away. Remember you will need to make sure you are not breaking the law when you are stashing your medication. If certain drugs require prescriptions, seek out a lawful -over-the counter alternative that could get you through the emergency in a pinch.

The first thing you should do, depending on your spending power, is to get yourself a proper emergency medical kit. These range in price. You might just want to assemble your own, based on your own particular circumstances and needs. Here is a basic list of supplies:

Alcohol/ peroxide

Antibiotic wipes

Latex gloves, or if someone is allergic to latex, nitrile gloves

Sterile dressings

Antibiotic ointment

Burn ointment

Adhesive bandages in a variety of sizes

4" x 4" Gauze

Bottle of saline

Eye wash solution

Thermometer

Syringes

Asthma inhalers, insulin, heart medicine, catheters, extra bottles of oxygen if there is someone who has a problem breathing.

Insect repellant

Aspirin or non-aspirin pain reliever

Anti-diarrheal medication

Antacid

Laxative

Other first aid supplies:

Scissors

Tweezers

Tube of petroleum jelly or other lubricant

Neosporin and fish antibiotics

Sambucol

Super ViraGon

Remember to check to make sure your expiration dates are more than two years.

Here are some websites that you can go to get ideas:

www.americanpreppersupplies.com/Emergency_Medical_Supplies_27.html

www.prepper-resources.com/medical-supply-kits-and-planning/

www.stormsurge.noaa.gov/preparedness-supplykit.html

www.fema.gov/media-library-data/1390846764394-dc08e309debe561d866b05ac84daf1ee/checklist_2014.pdf

As mentioned above, if you had to spend an extended time in your safety location and getting medical help was not an option, making sure you have some medical supplies on hand is a must. A word about fish antibiotics: In a desperate situation, if someone is injured, or has an infection and needs antibiotics, this might be a last resort. You should do your research and make sure that you buy the best products available for your family's safety.

Here is a link to purchase fish antibiotics:

www.campingsurvival.com/fishantibiotics.html?p=2

Here is a link to purchase a medical kit:

www.campingsurvival.com/firstaidkits.html

You can also go to Amazon.com and enter first aid kit in the search bar, and you will have a wide range of options to choose from. Now that you have your safety plan in place, as well as a stocked pantry and medical supplies, you are now better prepared than most. Now let's take a look at personal and home security.

Chapter Five: Personal and Home Security

Depending on where your safety location is, you will have to ensure that your spot is defendable to the best of your ability. If you are like millions of regular people, your home is located in one of two places: an apartment or a medium-sized detached home. If you are single, there are some decisions you can make fairly easily about your own needs, but if you have a family, then you will need to sit with your spouse and have an honest discussion about what everyone will be comfortable with. I say this because when you are thinking about defense, then you will have to decide where you want to be on the defense continuum. You can start with no defense, non-lethal, lethal, or a combination of lethal and non-lethal capabilities.

If you are the type of person who does not like weapons, then you will have to make the choice that when the bad times come, you will have to get creative in taking care of your personal safety, without the use of a weapon.

Let's look at this scenario. If you have made that decision, then maybe you would like to start reading about or taking a self-defense class. Depending on your location and your pocketbook, you will have to work out how to get the best bang for your dollars. There are a lot of self-defense manuals. If you rely on manuals and DVDs, you will have to practice on your own and hope that you are getting the techniques right. If you practice with your spouse, then at least you will be able to judge if the techniques are effective or not.

You can also make sure that your doors and windows are hardened. Do you have a plan in place that can make your doors and windows extremely difficult to break in? There are a range of cheap ways to harden your doors and windows. You can buy pieces of 2 x 4s to secure across the door, or nail up plywood, which can be used to brace both windows and doors. Some people will go as far as placing a sheet of metal behind the door, along with heavy 2 x 4 beams.

You can create a safe room, also called a panic room in your home or apartment. A safe room is a room hardened to be very difficult for the attackers to break in. You will have to hope that the room does keep them out, and that they will eventually go away. If you are planning a safe room, then it should double as your real pantry. You should have a secondary pantry, so that if someone was to break in, they would find those food stores, get happy, and run away. Meanwhile, you would be able to emerge not only alive and unhurt, but with most of your supplies intact.

Let's make this clear; the food that you keep in your cabinets and fridge should be your diversionary stash. If you can, you should make sure that your main stash is well concealed.

If someone was to break in while you were away, you can hope that they would locate the easy-to-find food and leave.

The best scenario is to hide and avoid any confrontation, and this should be your plan, even if you are armed. Remember, your job is to stay concealed and under the radar during the time of trouble. You should never make anyone aware of what you have, and have been doing. You will find that it will only make you a potential target if things get really bad. I would advise everyone reading this to watch the Twilight Zone episode "The Shelter." It shows what happened when a prepper tells his non-prepper friends about his bomb shelter, and how they attacked him and his family when there was a threat.

Let's move on to the middle of the continuum: You are armed with non-lethal weapons. Now this in itself is a misnomer, because all weapons are lethal under the right circumstances. Maybe you have a baseball bat, mace, or a Taser. Maybe you are thinking about getting one of these to use for self-defense. Baseball bats are of course available everywhere, while Tasers and mace, however, may not be available or require that you understand the laws where you live.

Certain cities and states do not allow citizens to own these self-defense deterrents. You have to make sure that you know the laws of your town, city, and state. You also have to make sure that you follow the law when you purchase the items, and keep all your paperwork in an accessible place. Tasers and mace should be stored in a quick access safe, especially if you have children in the house. You should never leave any weapon unattended. Weapons should be either on your body, or locked up in your quick access safe. If you know you are a careless individual, or if you have a personal philosophy of disbelief that an accident will ever happen to you with your weapon, then you should not get one. Having any weapon in your home is a huge responsibility. The only way to ensure that you will not have an accident is to make sure that every time you handle the weapon, you do so with extreme care. I will list the NRA gun safety rules later in this section. Memorize them. Tasers and mace should be handled just like firearms, because they can hurt people if used incorrectly, causing serious injury and pain.

Practice with your Taser and your mace. Make sure that you know how to discharge them under stress. This is as far as some people are willing to go. We will now move onto the other end of the continuum: Firearms.

I will be the first to say it. We all have the right to bear arms, but not everyone should own a gun. Gun owners have to be the steadiest, most law-abiding citizens on the planet. Gun owners never get "gun courage" and go looking for trouble, or running into danger needlessly. Gun owners understand the huge responsibility they have when carrying, handling, and using a firearm. Most people who arrive at the decision to own a firearm for self-defense know that, after searching their soul, they are able to take on the responsibility and risk of exercising their second amendment rights. They know that the minute they show their weapon in self-defense, their lives will change forever.

Most preppers will have one or all of the following four firearms in their possession. (1) Shotgun, (2) Hunting rifle, (3) Semi-automatic rifle, (4) Handgun. If you are thinking about protecting your home or property, the trusty shotgun can get it done. The following three shotguns are great for home defense: Remington 500, Mossburg 500, and the Winchester SXP. All these models are good options. There is nothing that sends a clearer message to a home invader than the sound of racking a shotgun. You should purchase the best ammo for home defense, meaning ammo that reduces, but most likely will not completely eliminate wall penetration and is potentially less lethal. Some suggestions for your shotguns may be No. 1 or 00 buckshot, birdshot, or rubber slugs. All ammunition will go through walls so you have to be extremely careful what you aim at. You should do your own careful research and make sure you have the correct shells that fit your needs and comfort level.

As far as hunting rifles go, I will list three rifles that would be great for hunting and pest control. They would also come in handy if you had to keep people off your property at a distance. These three are under $500: (1) Ruger American Rifle, (2) Marlin XL7, and the (3) Savage Axis. These rifles can be used for self-defense as well.

Now we will move on to the controversial semi-automatic rifles. These are the rifles that are called assault weapons by the uneducated media. These rifles can be used for hunting, self-defense, and pest control as well. There are rifles more expensive than the three listed here, but these have been given high marks for their versatility. With these rifles, the bullet is fed automatically into the chamber and can only be fired by pulling the trigger. This is an easier rifle to use because you do not have to manually load the round each time to fire it. Any version of the AR-15 comes immediately to mind. Smith and Wesson's M&P 15 Sport and Ruger's Mini-14 are all great, versatile weapons.

Finally, we will take a brief look at handguns. Many communities will require that you have a pistol permit before purchasing a handgun. Make sure you understand all the lawful requirements and follow through the application process. When you are granted your pistol permit, you can then go out and purchase a pistol or revolver. Some permits will limit you to just your home, while others will give you permission to carry your weapon concealed on your person. Make sure you are fully compliant with the law. You will also have a decision to make on your first handgun. Will it be a revolver or a pistol? There are certain advantages to both. Revolvers are pretty basic firearms. They are easier to load, fire, and clean. Cons are that they may not be as concealable as a pistol. Pistols have certain advantages; they carry more rounds, and are easier to conceal. Cons are that you have to really know how to fire the weapon and be familiar with it, and pistols are more difficult to clean. I will not get into what handgun to get. If you do get a handgun, you should be very practical about it. It's all about your needs and what you can handle. You will read many articles and chat with a lot of people who are very insistent about what they believe is the best way to select, carry, and fire a firearm, but you will have to read through and take the nuggets of wisdom that you can find. Select the firearm that you are comfortable with and fits your needs, and above all you should be able to hit what you aim at. For handguns, hollow point bullets are usually the best ammo for home and personal defense. Make sure you do your own research and buy the best ammo for your own needs and comfort level.

If you buy a firearm, you have to do your homework and practice safely with it. Above all, you now will have the huge responsibility of being a gun owner, and gun owners cannot be careless. Take as many classes that you can about using your firearm. At all times remember the four rules of firearm safety:

(1) Always treat every firearm as though it is loaded.

(2) Always point the muzzle in a safe direction.

(3) Keep your finger outside the trigger guard until ready to shoot.

(4) Always be sure of your target, what is in front of it and behind it.

You can find the NRA gun safety rules by following the following link below:

http://training.nra.org/nra-gun-safety-rules.aspx

So we now come full circle in our discussion of home defense. Your safety location should be as hard a target as you can make it. You will have to decide and come up with a plan of how to defend yourself and your family, in case your safety location gets attacked. Everyone in your family should be on board and understand the plan of action. Depending on your location and your own comfort level, you will decide how and what you will use to protect yourself and your family. Whether it be a safe room, baseball bat, Taser, mace, or firearm, you should make sure you are okay and well drilled on how to use your deterrent of choice.

Chapter Six: A Few Last Words on Your Personal Emergency Plans

In this manual we have looked at how to design your family's emergency safety plan and how to get yourself started on the road to a quick emergency prep. We discussed how to get your pantry started, store water and medical supplies, and how to make sure that your important papers and insurance are secure and up to date. We also discussed steps to take in order to defend your family and yourself, including how to harden your safety location and some basic ways to arm yourself in order to deter an attack.

If your finances allow, you should be able to follow all the suggestions in this guide and become prepped in as little as two to four weeks. **Week one: Sketch out your safety plan discuss it with your family. Week two: Get your pantry going. Week three: Get your medical supplies together. Week four: Harden your safety location.**

If you are not able to do much because of financial issues, then take your time and do what you can. You might not be able to do everything written here, but you can do some, and some is better than none. There are many scenarios that can unfold, causing mass chaos and danger to you and your family. It is up to you to be prepared the best you can.

There are other things to think about as well, like buying a small camping propane stove so that you can cook food and boil water. You may want to buy what's called a waterBOB so you can store water, and LifeStraws so that you can drink water from almost any source. Having a Travel Berkey Water Filtration System is also a good idea. You can look these items up and research them on Amazon.com or other shopping sites. You should also know where the fresh water sources are where you live. Remember, if there is no electricity for even 2 or 3 days, then you will most likely lose water pressure. That means no running water in your home, and nothing to flush the toilet. If you are living in a crowded city, then that will be a real problem.

If you live above the ground floor in an apartment building, and the elevator doesn't work, you may have to work out some problems getting to and from your apartment.

You should always keep your car's tank at least half full. If you have an emergency propane stove, then you should have at least one full propane cylinder. Also, in terms of communication, how do you communicate with your loved ones when there is no cell phone, internet, or land line service? You may want to think about getting a couple of powerful walkie talkies, especially if you and your family live and work within five miles of each other. There are many solar chargers available to charge your cell phone and laptop. You can find them at any electronic store or on Amazon.com.

Make sure you have a good tool kit, and a couple of fire extinguishers in your home. You should also get a decent battery or hand-cranked radio so you can tune in to any emergency broadcasts if the television and internet is down. You can use the two links below, one from the Homeland Advisory Group, and the other from the NOAA Weather Radio All Hazards web page. Find your state, city, and town, then look up the local emergency frequency closest to you.

www.homelandag.com/blog/2011/02/look-up-your-local-emergency-radio-station/

www.nws.noaa.gov/nwr/coverage/station_listing.html

Write it down and keep it somewhere you won't lose it.

You should also have a survival bag in your car. Make sure you pack the things you may need to get through a day or so on the road. What if you are stuck on the highway, or at work and you can't get home? What if you have to abandon your car and you have to walk home? What if walking home will take a day or more? What if you have to quickly leave your home and you are on the move to another location? What if you can take your car, and what if you can't? Your go-bag in your car should be light enough, but stocked with the necessary supplies to sustain you or your group for a few days. So when you are putting your go-bag together, you should think through every possibility.

So if the scenario was play out that you are in your safety location and you are bunkering in, and you can't leave your home at least for a few days until the authorities clear up the emergency, you could be monitoring the situation and staying safe because you have looked ahead and are prepared. As previously mentioned, other questions you may want to think about include: Will you let other people know what you are doing? Do you have likeminded friends who would like to set up a network to share information and assist if you need help, or are you going to go it alone? If someone shows up at your doorstep what are you going to do? These are all questions that you, as one of the prepared, will have to answer. You should do so and come to a firm decision of how you are going to handle these situations before they occur. That way you can handle them quickly and with decisiveness when they arise.

If you are preparing as a family, everyone should know all the rules and expectations of the plan. Monitor the news, and keep yourself informed. There is a lot to learn about how to prepare yourself and family to handle emergency situations. You should always be open to learning something new. There are a lot of websites that can help you along your prepping journey, and you can meet likeminded people who can share tips and offer advice.

This manual was not written for the prepper who is already a pro. It was written for the person who just needs a place to start. There are a lot of other, more detailed, books available that are loaded with very in-depth information and advice. This manual was written to give the newly concerned person a few quick tips on how to get the process of emergency preparation going.

Here are some websites that offer good places to go for prepping advice and to meet likeminded people. I am not affiliated with any of these websites:

http://americanpreppersnetwork.com/

www.theorganicprepper.ca/

http://thesurvivalmom.com/

www.theprepperjournal.com/

www.askaprepper.com/

www.thesurvivalistblog.net/

There are many more out there that can help you become better prepared. Amazon.com also has many books on prepping that you can purchase and become better informed. I hope that this manual has given you the encouragement to get yourself going, and that you will begin your journey.

Important Checklists

Chapter One: Getting Started on Your Own Personal Preparedness Journey

(1) What am I prepping for? _____

(2) Bugging In Y/N Bugging Out Y/N

(3) Did I check pantry space Y/N Clean Home Y/N Clean Car Y/N

(4) I live in City Y/N Rural Y/N

(5) My neighborhood is Safe/Unsafe

(6) I know my neighbors Y/N

(7) My neighbors know me Y/N

(8) I am satisfied with my safety location Y/N

Chapter Two: Developing a Quick Emergency Plan

(1) I have talked with my family about our safety plan Y/N

(2) I have drawn up the safety plan Y/N

(3) Check all that you have done:

- o Cleaned organized safety location
- o Stocked supplies
- o Prepped vehicles
- o Created a list of emergency phone numbers and radio channels
- o Scouted neighborhood
- o Copied and stored all important papers off main property
- o Updated home and car insurance
- o Have extra cash at home
- o Hardened safety location
- o Learned/ learning self-defense
- o Family has made decision on firearms
- o Ran emergency drills

Chapter Three: Stocking Your Pantry (Take this list to the supermarket.)

Check off all you have bought:

- o Flour
- o Sugar
- o Baking soda
- o Baking powder
- o Olive oil
- o Rice
- o Powdered potatoes
- o Powdered milk
- o Boxed UHT milk
- o Canned corn
- o Canned soups
- o Canned tuna
- o Canned salmon
- o Canned hash
- o Canned vegetables
- o Canned corn
- o Canned tomatoes
- o Canned spinach
- o Coffee
- o Tea
- o Oatmeal

- o Salt
- o Pepper
- o Garlic
- o Onion
- o Ketchup
- o Honey
- o Packaged meals
- o Macaroni and cheese
- o Raman noodles
- o Raisins
- o Nuts
- o Peanut butter
- o Chocolate bars
- o Cocoa powder
- o Energy bars
- o Bottled water
- o Canned soda
- o Powdered soft drink mixes
- o Bags of ice
- o Toothpaste
- o Duct tape

- o Flashlight
- o Toolkit
- o Water purification tablets
- o Can opener
- o Garbage bags
- o Toilet paper
- o Unscented soap
- o Shampoo
- o Deodorant
- o Cough and flu medicine
- o Feminine hygiene products
- o Toilet paper
- o Paper towels
- o Hand sanitizer
- o Batteries
- o Candles
- o Diapers
- o Infant formula
- o Baby food
- o Pet food

Chapter Four: Medical Supplies

How stocked are you?

Check off all you have bought:

- Alcohol/peroxide
- Antibiotic wipes
- Latex/nitrile gloves
- Sterile dressings
- Antibiotic ointment
- Burn ointment
- Adhesive bandages (pack of various sizes)
- 4" x 4" gauze
- Bottle of saline
- Eye wash
- Thermometer
- Syringes
- Heart medicine
- Insulin
- Asthma inhalers
- Catheters
- Bottles of oxygen
- Insect repellant
- Pain reliever pills
- Anti-diarrheal medication
- Antacid
- Laxative
- Scissors
- Tweezers
- Petroleum jelly
- Neosporin
- Fish antibiotics
- First aid kit
- Super ViraGon
- Sambucol

Chapter Five: Home Security

Check all that apply, and all that you've already done.

(1) I am going with (A) no defense, (B) non-lethal, (C) lethal

(2) I have discussed it with my family, and I have agreed on type of home defense Y/N

(3) I have hardened doors, windows, all entrances to my safety location Y/N

(4) I have selected and purchased self-defense deterrent of choice Y/N

(5) I understand all the laws on how to own, and when to use my deterrent of choice Y/N

(6) I have purchased a quick access safe to store self-defense weapon Y/N

I have routinely practiced with self-defense weapon to know how it works and how to safely carry, secure, and store weapon Y/N

Chapter Six: A Few Last Words on Your Personal Emergency Plan

The Four Week Emergency Prepping Plan

(1) Week One: Write out my emergency safety plan and discuss it with my family.

(2) Week Two: Start stocking my pantry.

(3) Week Three: Get my medical supplies together.

(4) Week Four: Harden my safety location, and run my first drill.

Acknowledgments

I would like to thank Desiree Snyder for her editing services. I would also like to thank www.ebooklaunch.com for their cover art and formatting services. If you enjoyed this book, please leave an unbiased review on Amazon.com.